Ming Saves the Day

Written by Mary-Anne Creasy
Illustrated by Meredith Thomas

Flying Start
to Literacy®

T0363484

Contents

Chapter 1

When will it rain?

"Ming, do you remember when it used to rain?" asked Ming's mother thoughtfully, as she made breakfast.

They both looked out the window at the scorched, dry land. It was early, but already so hot that Ming's clothes stuck to her.

"Of course I do, Mum!" said Ming cheerfully. "And I bet it will rain again soon."

Ming's mother just shook her head and sighed. "I hope you're right," she said. "We've never had a drought last for this long before."

In the village where Ming lived, it hadn't rained for a long, long time. The sun beat down, hot and hard, all day long. The village was covered in a thick brown dust, and the water supply was running low. No one could remember the summer ever being so hot or so dry.

The village had a small dam where all the villagers got their water for drinking, cooking and growing food. The villagers had built a system of bamboo pipes so water could flow from the dam to the gardens where the crops grew. A fresh stream had always flowed into the dam, keeping it full of water. But without rain, the stream had dried up.

The villagers were worried that the water in the dam might soon run out. But Ming wasn't. No matter how bad things got, she always believed that everything would work out in the end.

"Okay, Ming," said her mother, taking her empty bowl. "It's time to move the pipes and fetch the water. Off you go."

Ming smiled, grabbed the buckets and pole, and ran out the door. First she had to collect water from the dam for her family, then she had to move the bamboo pipes around so that all of the different crops got enough water.

Chapter 2

Sickness strikes the village

The next day, Ming was shaken awake by her mother.

"Ming, you need to get the water quickly this morning. Mr Chen next door is not well, so you need to get some for him, too!"

She handed Ming the buckets and pole and opened the door. "Hurry, Ming!" she said anxiously.

When Ming reached the dam, she dipped her buckets into the water. She noticed that it was not as clear as usual and had a greenish scum floating on top.

"Hmm," she said to herself. "That's strange."

Lifting the heavy buckets onto her shoulders, she headed back home.

Ming took a bucket to Mr Chen first.

"Oh, thank you, Ming," said Mrs Chen.
"My husband is so sick. He needs this water badly." She gave her husband a big cup of water to drink.

"What's wrong with Mr Chen?" Ming asked.

"He has stomach pains, but we're not really sure," said Mrs Chen. "A lot of the villagers are sick, though."

"Don't worry," said Ming. "I'm sure he'll get better soon."

Ming went next door and gave the other bucket to her mother, who drank some water thirstily. "Phew, it's hot today, I needed that," she said.

"Yeah," said Ming. "I'd better go and move the pipes before it gets even hotter."

Ming walked toward the village garden. The hot sun blazed down and brown dust swirled around her, getting into her eyes and mouth.

As she walked past the dam, Ming gazed at the water. Usually the water was so clear that she could see the rocks and pebbles at the bottom of the dam, but not today. Ming also noticed that the rock in the middle of the dam was almost entirely out of the water. Usually water covered the rock.

"Wow, the water level has gone right down," said Ming to Mr Tan, who was on his way to fill a bucket.

"I know. It is very worrying," he replied.

"It will be okay, Mr Tan. We'll have enough water. There's no need to worry."

Mr Tan smiled and shook his head. "I wish I was as positive as you, Ming." And he watched as Ming skipped off to water the crops.

Chapter 3

A visit to the doctor

When Ming woke the next morning, the sun was high in the sky.

"Mum, why didn't you wake me up?" she called, sitting up in bed.

Her mother didn't answer.

"Mum?" Ming rushed to her mother's bed, where she still lay. She was clutching her stomach and groaning quietly.

"Ming, I need help. Get the doctor."

Ming rushed out of the house and ran as fast as she could to the next village, where the doctor lived.

"Dr Lee," she panted, as he opened the door. "My mother is sick. She has terrible stomach pains, just like half the people in our village. Please, can you help her?"

"It must be the water," said Dr Lee. "We had the same problem in this village. With no fresh water coming into our dam, the water got polluted and it made everyone sick."

"What should we do?" asked Ming.

"For now, you must boil the water before you drink it or cook with it. That gets rid of the germs. Tell everyone in the village."

"But that won't solve your problem forever," Dr Lee continued. "Your village needs to start looking for another way to get water, like we did."

"What do you mean?" asked Ming.

"Look around," said Dr Lee, pointing at the mountains in the distance. "We're surrounded by water – all the snow on the mountains! It's melting all the time and it seeps through the rocks. Some of it goes underground. The land is very dry and bare, so if you see some healthy green plants, it could mean there's water under the ground."

"Did you find some water in your village?" Ming asked Dr Lee.

"Yes, we did. We dug under some green plants, and we found a spring!"

"Thank you, Dr Lee," said Ming. "I'll bet we can find a spring in our village, too!" And she ran home as quickly as she could.

Chapter 4

Green plants

Ming burst into the house where her mother was still lying in bed and told her what the doctor had said.

"You're going to be okay, Mum. You just need clean water. I'll put some on to boil right now."

Then Ming ran from house to house, spreading the word all over the village.

As Ming was walking home, exhausted, she passed the dam. She walked over and peered into it. The water level had gone down even more and it was dark, green and murky. She turned around and looked at the snow-capped mountains, far in the distance.

"I bet some water from those mountains is under our village somewhere," she said. "I should try to find some healthy green plants because there might be some water under the ground where they are growing."

And that's what she did.

Ming looked all over the village for a group of healthy green plants, but all the plants she found were dead or dying, shrivelled by the sun and covered in brown dust. The only green plants were the crops, but they were getting water from the dam.

Ming sat down to think. A short while later, she heard a voice.

"Hello, Ming," said Mr Tan.

"Hi, Mr Tan," she said. "I'm trying to think of where I might find some green plants growing in this dry ground."

"It's funny you should say that. I thought it was so strange, but I noticed some plants just like that growing on a hill not far from here."

Ming looked up at Mr Tan in surprise. "Will you take me there?" she asked excitedly.

About ten minutes later, they arrived at the spot. Sure enough, Mr Tan was right. A group of lush, green leafy plants grew in the middle of a patch of dry, dusty land.

Ming smiled at Mr Tan. "I told you everything would work out," she said.

Chapter 5

Fresh water flows

After a few days, most of the villagers were feeling better. Ming asked everyone to meet her at the spot where the green plants grew. Ming explained what Dr Lee had told her, looking around at the villagers excitedly.

The villagers looked doubtful, but they began to dig under the plants. The sun climbed in the sky and the villagers panted and sweated, but Ming insisted they keep digging.

Then, finally, Mr Tan yelled out, "I've found it! Look, the soil is wet! There's water down here."

Everyone cheered.

"Now how do we get the water out of the ground?" asked Ming.

The villagers talked for a while and decided to build a system of bamboo pipes leading from the underground water supply to the dam. That way, the village would have a fresh supply of water flowing into the dam again.

The people all worked together. Some cut the bamboo, some split it in half and some dug the channels to put the bamboo in.

They worked on and on and on. It was a huge job. But no one gave up.

Soon the water was flowing down the hill and into the village dam. All night and all day it flowed. Slowly, the water in the dam rose and, as it rose, it became clearer and cleaner.

By the end of the week the dam was full.

The people gathered at the dam to marvel at their work. Each person scooped up a cup of fresh, clean water and drank it. When Ming arrived with her mother, the whole village cheered for her because she had helped them to find clean, fresh water.

"I told you everything would be all right," said Ming, smiling broadly.

And it was. From that day on, the villagers stayed healthy and, even during the longest, hottest droughts, there was always a supply of fresh water in Ming's village.

A note from the author

The idea for this story came from an old novel about a doctor who travels to a remote village where people are suffering from disease. They have become sick and some have died because their drinking water is polluted.

I combined this idea with information I found about bamboo. In many parts of Asia, bamboo grows easily, quickly and is very strong. Here, bamboo is commonly used to transport water. In Ming's village, getting clean water from another source is the important permanent solution to the village's water problem. The way they use the bamboo to bring the water to the village is simple but effective.